Sway

Sway

Tricia Johnson

atmosphere press

Contents

Wildflower Bloom

Sway

The soft rustle of cotton fabric
Brushing against the body, clothespins in hand
With gentle wind gusts
As the shirt slowly dries on the clothesline
Crows caw
Bright green leaves rustle
Honey bees humming along
Birds a happy chorus
Everything in movement
80-degree day
Clouds
Then sun
Then clouds again
Patterns and rhythms
Swinging in time
To the socks and pants and button-down shirts
Hanging on the clothesline
A smooth and comforting rhythm
The body smiles
And sways along to this hidden song

Vacation Song

Wide soaring vastness
A flat blue horizon
Raise your arm flat- move it parallel to the ground
It is a straight line
Defined, definite
Drowning in blues
Warm wind
Strong whistling wind
Birds singing at the break of day
I forget:
The warmth
The birds have gone away
The sweet smell of flowers
Moisture in my nose
Pain-free existence
Stress-free neck and shoulders
As there is nothing balled on my shoulders
And nothing weighing down my neck
I breathe vacation in, and quiet calmness, contentment out
A soft smile marks my mouth
No jaw clenching, shoulders hunched, cheeks taught
Does vacation sing to my soul? yes
Does vacation move my spirit? yes
It's moist pleasurable, carefree nature robs my anxiety away

Traveling Between the Two

One foot on the ground
One foot in the air
Traveling between the two
Part of her grounded
Part of her soaring
She leans further back
In the striped sling chair
Nothing is clear
Many unknowns
But the moment is here
Tan colors, yellow pine wood
Soft gray porch, white rail
Purple cone flowers
Daisies gone to seed, blacktopped, green bottomed
Storm clouds building, closer yet
Molded into the thick air of humidity
Late summer hour
Come to pass slowly
With languid moving thoughts
Wrapped around the placement of one's feet
And the movement of the soul in this physical world of heat
A helix between tangible and nothingness
Limitless
The whirring of arms spread out circling in speed irrelevant of time
The mind's eye view of flying- simply sublime
Silver maple seed gyrocoptering down
In dappled light of sunshine

Sun Therapy

Wind, creates curls of skin, bumping
Through the leaves
Rush, shush, hear
Red among purple, smile
Buttercream yellow
Backyard cackle
Guineas talking
You feel so much
Hear so much
It slips around you
High high bird
Low back wind
Car left bank
Chimes cascade, simple bits of melody
Hat off wind strewn hair
Sun therapy
Outside summer afternoon
Cotton hammock paradise

Cells

Meadow sweet
Tall seeds of grass
Daisies
Buttercups set the table
Dewy drinks for tiny beetles
Deep wind chimes catch the breeze
I am near and far
I travel with wind in the Bradford pear
I dance and spin with bird songs fair
My fingertips trail upon the blades
I walk light as air
My sky unfilled of cloud
Clear light sapphire blue
The green hill looks resplendent
The gentle mounds, no sharp edges
Sweet smell, wildflower bloom in Pennsylvania
June has come
Erupts with pleasures, begins
Summertime dreams, songs, realized
Atmospheres
Lean back tilted head to sky
Rise of foot to table
Slow down take it in energy
Invades every cell in I
Listen, feel, succumb
Till you are numb dreaming along
A slow hum of song drifts lazily out, it is I,
A simple song of happy
Light breathy gone of air

Warmth

The birds have nested in the eves
In the coral purple house
How many babies would we see?
If we but dared to take a peek
The sun was muted upon waking
And now it emerges vibrant
Compelling, it will heat up the day
Brew the storms headed our way
It is so very common
As I looked out and saw the peonies blooming
That the June storms should come
The humidity is pungent
Thick breathing
Always sweet birdsong
Wind-chime
Warm breeze blew about
Fluffed the hair
Soft natural drying power
And I love it
The weather suits my soul today
Warm, languid, luscious breeze
Slow down feel see
Enjoy the wind
Clear the mind
Sit the feet up
Head back to stars
Crossed feet
Enjoy the meet

Shades of Green

The air is born of summer
Humidity
Sweet blossoms
Rush of blooms
Stems, leaves
Millions of shades of green
Emerald to peas
Dark spinach to pale lima
So many choices to be seen
In early June everyone sings
All hum along
Spin wide hair undone
Palm to ground
Hush the sounds of bustle in the brain-centered once again
Will we see a severe storm?
Will they pass by?
Rain thick and heavy?
You could drink the air
A million sweetnesses won
I see the beauty
I take it in kneel in clover
Smell its sweet spicy scent
Palms to ground
Greet mother nature
Connect soft grass between fingers
Tease the tops of hands
I am wealthy once again

Nestle

Meet me in the tall grass
We will settle in its hidden places
Nestled with mother earth
Daisy decorations
Sweet air
Beyond compare
Wild rose rush
Heady perfume
Lay back watch the sky
Arms rest under-head
Simply gaze, one
Stay awhile
As the fronds of seeded grass
Wave softly
Let us dream away this day
Eyes wide open
Blue topaz to gray-blue
Inside this curved out hollow
Wild greens trail around about
Upwards buttercup yellow
Deep in the green of meadow
Afternoon brightness filters
Falls gently on the watchers
Seeking sweetness illuminated

Summer Rain

The rain is welcome
The dry so arid
Puff of smoke fine soil
The earth is thirsty
To bathe in the sky's bounty
Leaf upon stem on flower
Everything holds its breath
Until the first hint of breeze announces the come storm
Rain on skin
Empowerment
Born

Traveler

Run away with the breeze
Through the perennial garden
Touch the mountain bluet
Spy the daisy budding
Tiptoe through the fresh grass
Tickle the legs in the tall field
Seeded bending north

Fly away across out reaching
Feeling the power, hot summer sun
Close the eyes and fall back
Grounding in the lawn
Eyes up looking through the leaves
Dappled sky, sun

The energy expands encompasses all
Connected caretakers one
Joyous welcome arms embrace
The sacred space of our
Feel the beauty, light, power
In the fresh southern breeze

A time of plenty in the open wild
Rush out, breath in the audible peace
Palms open receive
And give share in the bounty
Of promises keeping and growth steeping
To the color of amber

Amongst the In-Between

Humid cricket breeze
Geranium scarlet petal falls
The forest plays with wind, sings the rush
The air breathing water
The garden moist damp shade
From morning rain

The sky pale gauzy layered blue
Racing quickly eastward
Faded sling back chair
Feet upraised
Book in hand
Pen across page
Summer glory day

Wind-chimes serenade
Bird insect songs
The morning so alive
Swirls of wind mix the trees
The sun brightens up
And eases on playing through the clouds

Too much inside for me?
Hidden away from raging heat?
Sadness dims the wisdom
20 years ruled by children
The spinning comes undone
What is the spinning for?
What direction to take?

A moment to breathe
See a sense of clarity
Arms out to sky and air
Simply float along and be
The rays of sun on cloud dipped meadow
The hawk on winds unstable glided
The race of cotton cloud
Late daisy bloom
Emerald hummingbird
The smell of fall of yellow leaf
With summer tree frog
Blue jay winter bird
Amongst the in-between
Seasonal shift and pull
Fly away jet plane
A magical new beginning

Paint the Heavy

The rain may form
The sky deems it so
Grey to dark blue
Forming on top of you
A mix of day
Nighttime haze
Your eyes glaze
And see nothing
Ill-timed darkness
Mixed up emotion
Fat raindrop
Shatters the page
Your soul cries too
Silent prick to eye
Unstoppable weather drifting by
Pop-up storm of emotion
Clouded by such devotion
Fingertip outstretched to sky
Paint the heavy
Through to bright-eyed blue
Promise keeping
True

The Sweet of Growth

The morning is magnificent
The sun brilliant comforts us all
Fingers sweeping
Keeping us all reaching
Turn of head to sky
The crow calls with partner
Everything sings to stop
Notice witness
The grace that exists in nature
The hummingbird
The bumblebee
Call of hawk
Flit of songbird swoop
Graceful cat
Curl of new frond opening
Cirrus cloud shape of feather
Goldfinch
Half-moon present
Blue Jay call
I am not alone in this moment
Quick flight orange butterfly
The trees speak of change coming
I listen, see, know it so
Inhale the sweet of growth

Enchanting Morning Walk

Up to move
To walk, crunch of gravel
Bird of flight above head
Snake glisten road warmth, startle
Squirrel dances off through woods
The shade captures the walk from the east
The direction south
Uphill
Quiet to sounds of people
Crickets, grasshoppers, woodland flyers
Songs not heard in cities
In cars rushing down the hill
It is the walker, the witness
Bright purple, pure blue, gold flowers
Line the way
Greet the sun, the day
It is early, the wind is still
The dew sharp
The mind in magical connection
The moon, the sun share the sky
Stop, praise the magic
Sun warms the back, moon the soul
Enchants the morning walk

Dripping out There

Lower the film
To hide the sun
To shield the heat
To preserve the room
To breathe the air
To aid the lungs
From the dripping out there

See the light
That filters the fall
Soft as buttercream
That cools the face
Awakens the body
Drys the sheen
Of perspiration

Hide away from heat
The driving summer kind
That steals the breath
Buffers the mind
Boils the body, the air
The tendrils of hair
Suffocates the gasping
Robbing the fair

Smile to the curtain
To the closed window ledge
To the cool air pouring
Up the side wall vent
The silent rush of wind
Sweeping past the toes
To the mouth that smiling knows
The reprieve from hot, just there

Expectant

Surrounded by a room full in the open
Sky-high, miles wide
Movement beside green tendril flutter, peripheral vision
Fragrance falls brushes by the present
Soil nutrition, open-air freedom
Happy?
Happy waving observation?
Natural liquid hydration
Drops of rainfall cleansing deep
Caress of heaven falling cumulous calling, piled high cotton ball
clouds
We have moved we are outside
The natural order of growing
Humid cloak covers the fronds
Wind tousles the wide green leaf
And sun
Bright white intensity
Urgency
Summer pregnancy
Everything, all flourishes
Beautiful heat sent, long light growing days
And the plants stand tall
Stretch out
Bear flowers fruit growth
With the out-of-doors inspiration

No Physical Being

My floating deck of shade
An oasis of daydream possibilities
Sleeping napping wicker marked leg
Green leaf floating across the sky fade
Chasing windblown, bent over pines
Ride along the southern strewn sky
A pool with a deep reflection, lakes ponds ocean
The birds from tropical destinations
Eyes closed, float upon the warm wind
Nobody, no heavy, no physical being
A breeze stirred tendril of dandelion blond hair
My dreamy marigold, snapdragon land
Fairy lilies waiting in the stands
Nesting birds swoop dive and dip
Sing songs happy wobbly chirps
Close eyes, the sea?
The breeze?
Fly away visits of mind
On this floating deck imagination-driven ride

Soft Pearl Sky

Pearl soft sky
A promise of rain?
A renewal of moisture?
Saving the dry cracked soul
Opaque and lovely
Gentle, after fierce fiery heat
Humidity that wound about
Pulling tightly at the ends
To today
Where the world is folded loosely
Singing a melody
Merry in nature
Not swift
Not hold your breath fast
A pace that measures the ebb and flow of a more natural rhythm
The busy holiday time
The high flying crackle pop boom time
Lights in showers of umbrella sprays
Excitement whirling
To today, recapture the subtle
Pointed movements of being
Happy in the recovery
Of a soft pearl sky

Catch the Fleeting Bright

The sun illuminates
Golden graceful stay
Alights the simple glorious
A sparkle, a purple shade
Yellow band of circle
The sun erupts from cloud bank
A welcome back friend
Makes the mundane magnificent
All the tiny intricacies known
The sun calls to everyone
Blesses all with growth
Enlightenment
Catch the fleeting bright
The beauty found in light

Essence

Fly away in wind chime land
Music made by fancy
Whimsical deemed, released
Sparkling glittering pieces of me
Reflections of shattering sunlight
Smoke and wave, fire in the air
Of all of this that weights the souls
To spin and dream things unseen
Wrapped in silk ribbons
Alive with the breeze
Aquamarine in color essence
Blue of water, light of gold
Arms out marveling
Feet off ground traveling
Freedom unbound
Know not a sound, just rush of wind

Raw Summer Magic

I am green sloping hills, round
Half circles
Smoothed by millions of years
Meadows of wildflowers
Golden, purple, ivory
Rustle of leaves, wind caught, stir
Aqua sky, cotton texture cloud drifting
Aspen quake
Pink zinnia bloom
I choose of what I am, whom
I am rural Pennsylvania
Crayon yellow daylily
Northern country
Teasel in bloom with goldfinch resting
Monarch butterfly passing through
Speckled fawn watchful momma
Flick of white tail and gone
I soar with hawks
Ride the waves of treetops
Rush along the creek beds
I am gray stone in all the colors of shadows
I smell sweet as aster
Fresh crushed grass, baled hay
I am warm southern breeze, feather touch toes, ears
Birds song, chatter, trills
I am warm honey color taste
Thick on tongue
Sweet layers discovered
Brush back sheer back of hand
Vision fills eyes

I am blue sky filled with whip cream dollops
Pure raw summer magic

Pumpkin Decorum

Meteor Shower

Bright white slash
Brilliant against deep endless black sky
A glimmering patchwork of stars
Sparkle twinkle wink of an eye
Then fierce firework display
Skipping into atmosphere
A child's toy spark maker
Skipping down the drive
A magic wand grants a wish
Swish of sparkle light arcing
Then gone
Twenty plus more
Curled cocooned blankets
Against damp grassy soil
Magic hushed giggles cheering
Natures show
Celebrations
Fleece coat and hood
Jean flannel quilt
Someone is skipping stones of light
And we are watching still

Suspension

You wake up to nothing
The quiet is absolute, you are empty yourself
The air is crisp
The night black
You listen in vain
Straining to hear, yet you know you will not
Find the crickets
Find the summer frogs
Find the coyotes yipping, trees bending, leaves sighing
Find the owl moving

Sound carrying down the gully and away again
In a pattern you cannot find
It is as if the world has stopped.
No breath
No wind
The noises of summer have moved away
To where?

You lay still in bed
Listening
Then breathe in this change of season
This quiet lacking any movement
This early morning, late night
Mystifying sensation
That there is nothing else

Everything holds its breath
And you wait for the exhale
Seconds feel like hours
You hold your own breath
There is no hearing
There is just suspension
In thought, movement, noise
You are caught and digest the fact
It is autumn
It is quiet
It has come

Walk

Grey, sparkle white frost
Pink cheeks and nose
Cold fingers, purple
Smoke gliding out of chimneys
Quiet morning
Fog
Brilliant perfect circle sun
Pushes back fog and frost
Lines emerge along sunlit paths
Walking
Cold air in
The smell of fall
Warm air out
The chill felt through fabric
Moves to sweat along the back of a scarf wrapped neck
Happy puppy barking welcome
Warm black fur in fingers
The sun has just enough warmth
The walkway glistens
The mums are fading
I feel happy

Autumn Pause

Change is coming
Empty house change
Color orange change
Brown tone earth
Warm light
Cozy
Color
Alone
Home
Untalking
Quiet
Pause

Mosaic

I travel with the wind up the slope
Through the forest of White oak
The rush and sigh of leaves my wake
My soul glides, to find a safe place
Away from all the world's turmoil
Politics, policies, health and change
Negative tentacles, that leave a stain
I am wind in undercurrents, through the forest floor
Under over logs and twigs, last year's foliage
Amongst the rocks and boulders, slide upward
Racing for the heights, headed South
Emerge straight up to clouds, splayed hand design
Up
To chase the streams of light and sun
Up
To relinquish the pain and ache of body-mind
To play with particles, encasing my body
The colors of indigo, tangerine, and gold
Shades of brightness caress my soul
Weightless wonder at it all
Given emerald green and
I am seen once more
Rich damp soil in hand
Life, earth the divine
The fire of inner being, riding the element of air
To rain down again, droplets of water
Release translucent warm salty orbs
I am the elements and something more
The unique points of rainbow, sparkle through crystal suspension
Colored glass pieces, mosaic of me

Wink

One red leaf on my maple tree
Winked out as I walked by
I said hello, introduced myself
Thanked its crimson glow
A nod toward change
A season swooping in
The center glimpse of rose
Wrapped in the nature of green

Frantic Energy Moving

The light is indirect, cold filled sky, filters
The breeze twists the tops of trees, rearranging
They sway in multiple directions, of play?
Of awakening? Shaking off the still hot days?
Exploring the 70s of early autumn
Look up to watch the display
The leaves seem dark upon the gray
Frantic energy moving, blowing the walking me down the road
It is brisk in all movement
Invigorating, accepting
Cleansing away the negativity
Such possibilities, spin embracing me
Eyes closed walk forward savor
This moment of movement wrapped in gold

Wind Shower

The wind races through
Cleanses the deepest you, clear the debris
Heartbeats of vision
Directions given
Sweeps away the shadows
The unknown unseen darkness
Inhale always with eyes closed
To block one sense to fill another
To focus on that rush of air
Through nose down throat
Expand lungs taste the air
Expel
Arrive here
Eyes burst open
Natures salvation
September wind morn

Elemental Fire

Tucked away
The beautiful at play
The view, the valley
The crow song echos
Grey kitty cat, open window
Long fur, gorgeous white
The fall is coming
Maroon grasses, tan grasses
Goldenrod heavy blooms
Pink tinged leaves soon to change
Maple dotted with red
Elms yellow arm
It is on the horizon calling
Autumn beauty telling
Cool morning fog in valley
Sunlight treetops, hilltops
So many insect songs
The soul is gold, red and orange
Warm with fire
Fly away magic's invitation come

Shallow

I do not wish to think so deep
My mind an ocean's keep
Dark oasis caught spinning, spun, undone
For quiet meditation's sake
I do not wish to delve
Discover new to ponder
To stay light float about
Down thistle drift
Merriment of wind direction unknown
Let the steep focus filter past
I am shallow ankle width breath
Seasonally swept away
Pink blush autumn flush
Surface light kissed wave of movement
I do not wish to dive today
My mind shall float instead

Sweet Gentle

With wind and sun, the falls begun
Gentle chimes rings clear
And the stress sails away
Leaves you free
To feel the sun
On face and cheeks
Wisps of hair affected
Tiny tangles, ring the head
A yellow halo
A cat slinks in, sashays by
Mews a hello, with a trailing tail
The smell, fallen leaves
The feel, late burnt August grass
Warm earth, lovely
The sight, is closed eyes turned to sun, brightness, colored lids
A moment, fills months of empty struggle
Knees folded sideways
Skirt folded under
Amber lit sun
Open palms receive
Radiance Equinox gives
At last, the sweet soul again lives

A New Turn

I am running free
In poetry
Of my own hand
And mind
And soul

I explode with the wind play in the leaves
That have turned to autumn, shades in yellows

The oranges wrap around me
Release a smile at their beauty
Lit up from within
Fire my way forward
I live again in breaths shallow

Magnificent sky opens wide
Endless cobalt
Icy white, the spectrum
The color wheel spins
Welcomes a new turn
The eye rejoices

Enrich

Changing leaf colors
Speak a different song
The rush of wind altered
Does the yellow know this?
Or even the red?
The sun illuminates the subtleties
As some rush off to play
A final flutter whoosh
To ground to give back
To soil
To enrich
Feed, replenish
The life cycles of nature
My philosophy
Church, religion
I smile her way, breathe her fall scent
A new chapter begins
A new season sings
Fallen leaf
Damp, sweet earth

Fly

The wind roars
The house seems to stretch at the rush
Blow up from the inside
To hold
Hold fast
It is past
Golden leaves zoom by windows
The trees swirl
Up I look to see
Yellow oblong sun glint upon pale sky
Moving twirling upward
Can I fly too?
Travel in this dance?
Free to soar
Play along this Autumn day?
In a second of an instant
A glance heavenward
And I flew too
High to feel the bright sun
Light up my world glitter bright
The breeze my direction
A raw elemental connection
Simple
Air
Leaf
Free

Rocking Chair

Life can be joy
Wonder
Sight of leaf
Sound of chime
Heat of sun on skin
Cool air through nose
Rocking chair
Back porch
Torty cat
Underneath purr
Burgundy oak
Tangerine maples
Green grass once again sunlight on forest floor
Peeks out with fallen leaf
Rosehips
Red mum enjoy the weather
Warm southern wind
Kisses us, cheeks both right and left
Greets us fondly
Hawk sales by silently watching
Such beautiful bounty
Joy unfolds
In soul
In life once more
Step outside and find it

Pumpkin Latte

The pumpkins
Disappear by the night raiders
Quietly coming in
Sideways chew
Eating up the boy's spoils
Soon to start on decorations
I wait for first signs
Of chewing nibbles and footprints
And they will eat it all
All the seeds and pumpkin meat
It must be candy sweet
The deer make no sound
Simply enjoy their find
I do not actually mind
It is my fall decorum
But maybe something more
A gift, a harvest wonder
To forest dwellers
Savoring their own pumpkin lattes

Shakes Herself Dry

Traveling with the wind
Through the trees
Down the slope
Up the hill
Around the house
By the creek
In the pines
Waves the tendrils of willow
The earth shakes herself dry

One

Crescent waning moon
Sun far to east share the sky
November morning
Quiet
Far away traffic moves highway
Glimpse of slight frost creek bed
Damp dew-laden grass
Fresh mowed fall field
Tidy up for winter
Pause feel the sky
Close the eyes
Soft palm
Roll of earth
One

Quilts in Autumn Spreads

Turn the corner, face north
The wind curls down your body
You realize it is late autumn
The warm reprieve, unprecedented temperatures
Over

Your pace quickens to chase away the chill
That teases your fingers and exposed skin
Winter is coming, the trees barren
Tucked in with leaf blankets
Colorful quilts in autumn spreads

The runoff from yesterday's rain
Stops you, deserves a second glance
Is it frozen? Is that ice?
It flows in patterns reminiscent of cold

Your oak trees beckon
The sentinel your protection, watcher, wisdom
The second, up through branches
Up to sky your eye traces its reaches
Leaves catch the breeze wave
Slight to faster, there are fewer now
Change
From uncharacteristic warmth
To comfort of chill at normal
A walk in time of season

Glide

Cloud in sky day
But it lightens
A bit of hope dawns
Hushed away here at home
Nature
Walk
Leaf
Color
Project myself unto another
Sail away float glide
Hide away walk past
Beautiful chill
Warm coat
Pink
Girl
Smile
Quicken step
Breathe
Alone unwatched
Free

Elemental Lines

Late day slant of sun, wonderful warmth, half of face
Soon to pass beyond the hill
Long shadows cast, elongate
Crescent sun in the sky to east
Rising, filling with days that pass

Just light of sun kisses my face
Soft wind plays about my curls
Thistle dry, seeded out sway
With down of goldenrod, turned to gray
It is a late autumn time

The wind speaks up to tell the story
One day warm up, from southern direction
Fast high moving clouds, paint my blue sky
Slashes of gray-white color
Race along drifts, I cannot fly to touch
Only through mind's eye and dreams

Yet the cool earth, grounds my path
Strengthens the spirit, ties to now
Soft feet upon late verdant grass
Glistens of its own, in arching sun
Birds shelter and sing in corn crib, firewood barn
The wisteria, a shelter-playground, their movement a song
Wind chime resonates softly, triangular tones

I am brushed by quarter notes and elemental lines

The element air plays my hair
The fire warms my face
The earth holds me solid close
The water still illuminates

Night Air

Walking in the night air
Cold rain
Softly moves my hair
Fog swirls through the trees
The brown fall leaves
Shine bright rinsed
Mud pulls at my boots
Heels sinking past respectibleness
Alone
Silence, save flowered boots walking
Even brief excursions outside
Cleanse the soul
In passing

Light Captured Hexagons

Breakthrough

Sunlight
Piercing - bright
Is it because it has been gray all day?
In that fleeting moment, it blinds the sense of sight?
Your nose points toward it
You close your eyes from the stinging
And embrace the warmth you have missed
One breath, two and it is gone again
You are chasing rainbows of the sunlight
Winter's chill is here
Everything hides from the cold
Colors disappear
Shades of tan and gray
Sepia hues, if you are lucky
Sleep the slate filled world

Pine Tree

I am a pine tree
Moving with the breeze
Brushing by you as I please

I am sunlight, deep green
Graceful ballet
Sway with me

Head nodding to and fro
I am there, the branch
Let go

Eyes fixed, breathe
Slowed, mind
Living pine tree
Symbiotic love

Just Feel

Darkness, coolness faded starlight
Quiet, no sounds of movement
Insect, animal, us
A soft wet kiss to cheek
Startling familiar caress
Again, turn of head to see?
Where did you erupt from?
What direction are you?
And again intimate minuscule whisper of a touch
Delicate, turn of head skyward
Winter sweetness flakes of snow
Unseen in blackness caress the tired soul
Wake up the senses
Smile, giggle, lightness, young of heart
Close eyes just feel
Padded quiet foot puppy moving
The long-ago green blades of grass frozen fast
Nighttime walk in late autumn

Silent Flight

Featherlight winter kisses
Looking upward
Light captured hexagons
Up above
Illuminated in darkness
A bubble circumference
The rest black night
Low clouds
Quiet the world
A riot of falling snow
Soundless
Out you go to surprise
Its existence
Creates fresh awe every-time
Startled gazing up
Sweet gentle flakes
Brief kisses of cold
Gently caress your face to now
In the moment
Memorizing the held breath
Upward sightless gaze
Of silent flight of snowflakes

Northeastern Pennsylvania

Whimsical
Mesmerizing
Rapid backwards
Individualized crystalized
Energy from heaven
Atmosphere releasing
White geometric creations
Breathe in float away
Breathe out ride along, from north to south
Canadian wind of arctic origin
Great Lakes creations
Fleeting inch giving snows
Lake affect

Gently

Smell the cold
Feel it
Sense it
Pushing down
Mittened hands cupped
Upside down gently

Connections

Snow a silent friend falling
Scalloped edges, cirrus yarn
Quiet winter dog walking
Happy
Peaceful
Spruce green tree, natural element be
Moving quick then slow
Pulled along, up a slope
Spin in circles
Red tangled up with green
Peeling paint from birdhouse
Small footbridge
Witness the passerby
A crunch of ice
Underfoot
Connects them to earth,
To ground, to sky
The falling quietly snow

The Eyes are Cold

Even the eyes are cold
Crystal dry
Wide feeling
Exposed
Awareness at the new location
Dim view of beige
Three-week repetition
Familiar space
Familiar seat
Familiar face appears
The slow walk backwards begins again
Head turned glancing, seeing
Freeing the tired mind
Truth of line, written to recall
To forget the madness of then
Silver raindrop butterfly wings
Hilltops tree tops feather branch splay
Gravity fighting rise
Cherry pink cloud, float
Sun's western shadows falling
Lightening the midway turning point, warm creamy yellow
Palm up gazing hand, fingers light as feather
Soft curl, reach
Steam whipped high

Winter Minute

Foot crunch of snow
Ice frozen 19 degrees snow
Sunshine warmth on face
Juxtaposition
The noise of cold
The feel of warmth
Nothing else sounds, moves
It is simply you
Alone
Walking, forward
Toward the edge of the rolling hillside
You cannot see over
A quiet reflection? No
It is foot meets ground
Breathing, moment found
Nothing else
The why of the sound so massive in its moving
As you are there
Perfectly formed geometric crystal of snow, shattering
The silence
With your passing anchoring you to this second
This slide of foot
Explosion of sound
Sunlight face

Sliding into New

My life a hexagon sparkle
Caught up in gold
A moment of shimmer
Of clarity, of now
I am a color suspended
Watched, dazzle shine
It is winter absent of color
The color comes from inside
Small spark of fire
Resting with the weather
It will rise again
Soon?
Nesting time upon us
Covers drawn up
Flannel and fleece and wool
Warmth measures taken still
The sun is warm
The shadows cool
Scales tipping
Wind and brush of cheek
Change of season

Remembered Possibilities

Deep howl of wind
Down through the gully
About the house and away
Bass notes in a hurry
Surprising the passerby
Is it cold?
The blue ice says yes
Frozen water crystals floating
Hard packed old snow
Tells little
The sun lights my page
Its beauty well appreciated
Startled bent over
Look up relish the brightness as collect the dry firewood
Startles in its newness
After days of gray
Gray clouds and hills
Gray sky low to earth
Brilliant sunlight
Cascades, glitter about my hair
Lights up the inside with
Possibilities wide hands scoop up
Pass through open fingers

Sail Away

From stillness
To rocking
I move with the trees
Away out of body
In the air
At the top
Along the lacy branches
Gentle and strong
Bear the weight of bird
The brunt of wind
Hold my soul, embrace
The sleeping tree
The gray outline
The winter day
The wind at play

There You Are

And there you are again
Mediation in movement
Rocking away
Outline on sky
Tilt of head to left
Fly away too

Winter Moon

The moon and I face to face
The clouds separate
Around her full open eyes
She sees me
Through the colors
Grounds me to the earth
The clouds are moving fast
Flying south
As the geese earlier
An inverted V
Black sky, white orb
How is that done?
Everywhere overcast
Except just there
I stare on
Warm hands, palms
Pass up the inner workings
Mysteries of being
Breathe deeply in, release
Lighter
As the perfect crystals touch my cheeks
The fire illuminates
Its heat crashes with the cold

Deep with Life

Nighttime magic
Deep with life, quiet
Alone in the shelter of the full cold moon
Oak tree sentinels
Primal fire
Goodbye to past, cleanse
Fire cheeks, cold to sky
Soft white, blue-lit world
Pure snowflake caught in eyesight
Unrushing falling
Beautiful, hold my breath

Pleasantly Pink

Freezing song outside today
The cold drives deep within the bones
The chill to face and hands, toes
Winter has weeks to keep
Layers of snowstorms deep
Rough edges clumsy walk
Breakthrough sideways tilt
Crunch so very loud
As winter is silent now
The birds to bed
The squirrels to nests
Sweetly wrapped plump tails
The deer in the distance
So very brown on white
Watches, listens completely still
Then burst forth in movement
Across the wide expanse of field
I still, listen become the watcher
A gift of nature
So perfect the outline
And then to move, out of the cold
To find the warmth
Unwrap the scarf, the heavy boots
Cheeks still pleasantly pink

There

And there
There is the snow
The storm begins
Thin pieces transparent
Movement so small
You wait
And stare
For it to become significant
As the flakes grow fatter
Large ones with small
They seemed to be sure of this storm
Yet it kept you waiting
Beginning later than thought
It is the filling in snow
It promises to bury us deep
Soft layers over tough
Whisper over crunch
Silent storm
Marching in
Quick watch to catch its passing
Swirls in multiple directions
Before it settles in
For the long fall

Together

Face to night
Tilted upward
Cold feather white touches
Quiet noiseless
Calm
Silence of soul
Interruption of necessity
Creates wonderment
Time trace awe
A gift to realize the present senses
Revel in their luxury
Being alone
Yet together
Eyes closed
Softly catching snowflakes with face

Outside

Gray wings in gray trees
White flakes in gray sky
White ground trees anchored
In frozen
It is frozen
A frozen land in time flutter filter fall from the sky
Look straight up and you fly
Spaces unknown
Cold feather of flake
To face eyelashes cheeks and lips
Sweet softness of cold
And moving stillness

Pearl Gray Dawn

A snowstorm comes in so quietly
You wake up to the silence
And somehow your soul knows
Through that pearl gray dawn
That it is snowing
So much movement
So much falling
Yet nothing, no sound
Constant multitudes of energy
Whisper quiet
I love the silence of a snowstorm
It says just now
Be still, watch without hearing
See by the color of a cool morning bedroom
That it has begun

Melodious

Periwinkle

Bird song in circular motion
Ever turning to find its source
Impossible spring melody
Butter warm sun
Green, brilliance awakened
Colors, colors,
Periwinkle
Royal yellow
Red bud purple
Starving eyes, ravish the delight
Soil fragrantly cool, moist, and rested
The wind twirling about exposed necks, in raw silk smoothness
Decadent arrives the new season

Aloft in the Wind of Monday

The world outside is stirring with wind
Fingertip swirls on the tops of trees
Sunlight so bright
Spring green grass
Tiny growing leaves

I am spinning, floating
Carried along in thoughts deep within my mind
Gliding away in feather Christmas boughs
Aloft in the wind of Monday

Swaying mesmerized
Imagining weightlessness
Moving in the secret forest hides
Sunlight shadow passing turn brightness up
Electric swivel switch on highest setting

Hold on float away
Clasping fingertips
Arms thrown wide turning
Eyes closed head back
Being wind reborn

Ebb and Flow

I am:
    4

I am:
    forget-me-knots and more
    the summer breeze, wind chimes, birds of every color

I am:
    healthy new green leaves, plump on May rain
    surprise iris packages, unfolding shades of purple

I am:
    the smell of fresh-cut grass, phlox by the river
    pieces of me in all of this
    pieces of me tasting sampling these wonders of new

Do I leave as much as I take?
Small tendrils curling out wind caught like spider webbing?

Do we share this experience together?
They capturing the blonde-haired woman watching by?

We share fluidity of energy and pieces of me swirl on
with pieces of rainbow they

Shadows Bold

Sun makes shadows bold
Clear precise likes unfold
Blue sky miles wide
Melt away spring snow
Quickly now green grass show
Swiftly comes, swiftly goes
As sun keeps shadows bold

Working Pollen Legs

I am breeze
Spring green
Fresh, new
Breath

I am song
Spring bird
Happy, dancing on air

I am peepers
Awaking
From long winter sleep

Yellow dandelions
Downy cotton
Blowing
Yellow
Black
Fuzzy soft
Working pollen legs

Musical Blanket

The birds call
Is it all the same language?
Do the musical notes carry a riot of conversation?
We hear the melodies, not the words
They lift up, lighten, unfurl
To listening ears, grateful
To witness
Curl up in musical blanket

To Spring

Come pull me from my mind
Out of the tangle
Winters last tentacles
The nesting time is over
Deliver me to green blades
Golden trumpets
Chorus of flight
Coo and trill
Movement of water, bubble
Downward slope of stone and rubble
Fair sky, robin-egg blue
Born new to season

Kisses of Possibilities

Cool morning breeze
Drifts in about exposed nose, forehead, face
Rush gently and gone
Pleads a wake up song
Wet earth scent
Rain the night through
The grass turns to easter shades
In eyeblink time
Spring holds so much promise
Whispers it with the new growth, gifts it
To feast of eye
To each distinct sense exposed
After long winter silence
The smell of wet earth
The dance of worms
The trill and swoop of bird
Bud and blossom swollen trees
Soft pungent herbs to fingertips
The kisses of possibilities
Brush of cheek, hyacinth

Half of Me

My feet and mind at distance
One is here, one the other
Is it artistic, driven?
The quality of dreams walking
Immersed in the nature of now
The rapture of spring about
Squish deep in mud path
Green so bright my eyes sing
Half of me floats on, about
Half of me walks the yard path
Scattered as my daffodils
Golden thoughts scene at distance
Beautiful aroma stored
I am in the small wells of water
Strewn about the yard
The red bud blossoms, umbrella shape, dots to sky
The cold feel of puddles and mud
Through spring boot rubber
Individual blades of grass
Sharp in color
Half of me is lost to senses
Half of me slow in walking
Stiff of body, lack of breath
Around the curve, south by east
Heavy feet grounding

Flight

Away and back you travel by
Stir of lips
Kiss the sky
Still so watching
Cease of breath
Slight tilt of head
To west
Home of night
The flight
Is brief
The red is real
The feel
Is life
The wind in hand
Slight burst
Invisible
Known
In second
Minute
Past
One

Leaf, Unfolding

Come and play the day away my love
Fresh tiny leaf unfold
Step in line dance
Dip and glide about the air
Bare fair face to sun unknowingly become
The loveliness of sunlit day

Interconnected

Steep, slope of mountain almost 90-degrees
Yet you stand so straight and tall
Even high reaching arms
Spare no falls
Strong the character?
Strength of land
Roots deep through rocky soil
Bird and beast your family
Roots intermingling
Connected in earth; connected in air
As empty branches sway together
Wrapped around and through a tricky puzzle
Are you holding hands?
Dancing together? When the wind rushes past?
Braced by foot and hands
Ever making amends, for the foolish humans' pleasures
Yet not all are this
There is great gratitude given
Awe, inspiration seen amongst your red promises of spring
To paint this world alive
Growing, stretching
A choir of birds singing
And I am kneeling viewing
Your grace once more receiving

Science

The call is elemental
The periodic table
Building blocks of all that is, life
Pulls you from your tired sleeping home
Rushes you outside
The hum of life vibrates
Within, everything
And you need to join its song
Sweet pattering feet
Scatter by, a path well-trod
Buzz of working bee seems so loud
Is it because you have forgotten this tune?
It hasn't been played in so long?
It rumbles out past your heavy chest
Releases the weights of past
Eased along slowly
Lest you blow away quickly
Evaporate back to basics
Atoms of songs

Currents

From spring rainstorm
To snow accumulation
April weather like March
Laced up backwards
Warm, to sunny, to gray to cool
Not sure in direction
Simply riding the current of now

Red Wing Black Bird

Distinct call
My eyes switch direction
Search
You are orange, red, yellow?
Are you there?
Brilliant ebony fair
Top of white blooms
Hello beautiful
Its song a companion
Connection to deep within me
Mysteries
Mystical observations variations
As to the why, I know not
Silver white opal ribbon connection
Trace of finger, flown through air
The connection hums
The step is light
The smile wide, wild, right
Full deep breath
Life

Johnny Quill

The hazy low hung clouds of morning have decided to blow away
The shadows brighten on the page
Blue sky promise westward horizon
Has the chill run away? A bit of warm up for this day?
The snow bent daffodils need the warmth
A breeze to dry the soggy earth
Sunlight to lift the late snow blues, that came in late April
Lift up to blue, breathe, release
Seize the springtime, rejoice and live
The ground grows green
The flowers emerge yellow, golden johnny quill
A hyacinth pink
Sunshine yellow forsythia
Redbuds on trees bursting eager
The slow warm up sings in the blood of everything
Everyone
We are running with the water down the ridge
Singing with the robins, clear one-note songs
High vibrations stir the world to action
The resting time has done
And so this new world becomes

Buoyant

Budding pushing upward plants
Shoots so fresh alive
Offer such pure hope
In so many shades
Ruby red, maroon plum, lime green
So many dancing colors after months of shades in tan grieving
Resting retrieving waiting, now stretch out fingers feeling
Never cease to amaze
The growth in a day, in an hour of sunlight
In a minute of rain
It fills in the parched winter cracked skin
Smooths out the lives, blends the point to page
Magnificent, smiles tug the corners of your mouth
You hum along, a buoyant song
Dance with the rhythm of spring

Wind Song

How is it the dust billows in the wind
And the yard squishes beneath the feet?
Extreme dry to murky wet
The wind steals away breath
And the sun fires up the soul
Contrasts
Up rises the wind
Startles I, startles cat
Swirls around turret
Blast upward fast
Powerful, wait to hear a crash
With the train sound through the forest
Fast ruptures of air
Zoom about in which direction? I know not
My heart speeds along with it
My eyes try to follow
Invisible its nature
Its song loud, untamable
Oh to fly on that fast-moving train
Free windswept directionless be
Spirals along mountains, treetops
Grass valleys, how beautiful would it be
To know this fury

Lovely Touch

I am surrounded with the lushness of spring
360 degrees of birdsong
In a riot of keys, even an owl through the trees up the gully
The creek is rushing north
The downpours have passed
Again the owl calls a spring gobbler answers
What words do their voices convey?
Is it but a message they could share with us?
I feel it is happy
Warmth has returned, the sun is peeking out
Carefully pulling back the layers of clouds
A small aircraft flies overhead, it sets the course to summer
Nesting bird in grape birdhouse
Guineas chirping eating a merry tune
Two female cats of a similar color cannot coexist, shoddy truce
Staring eyes gone black, creeping
The dandelions are charging out
Loving the dancing bees touch
They have been hungry waiting
The multitude of song fills my cup
The brew is heady steamy aromatic splendor

Ripeness of Lemon Time

Playful yellow goldfinches
Flitter fly through the red bud
Quick racing seeing knowing
Chatting quarreling
Celebrating spring
Gray rain day
Their bright colors stream out
So vivid in play
The yellows have arrived
Golden dandelion
Goldfinch
Golden daffodils dancing in the wind
Yellow lightens the weight of my heart
Brightens the rain heavy gray days
Offers hope again
New seasons offering
Gifts of colors brightness knowing
I shall play in the yellow
In the golden growing
Gone from a thousand shades of beige
To ripeness of lemon, butter, banana split

Flush of Skin

I am the green vine unfurling
Fingers wide open curling outwards striving
Curiously seeing

Knowledge seeking
Creativity singing
Melodious rumpus of being

Sly sliding trilling
Opening to spring
Green, golden, everything

Awaken my center
My love, my splendor
Soft hands gliding
Flush of skin sighing

Gentle giving, taking sharing making
I am the green vine in springtime transcending

Silk Butter

To describe the state
Of unbeing
Mixed in half of two worlds see
The ethereal aura shades of pink?
Golden sparkles? shimmer, blink
Fill the gaze
To current
Look about window
Gray low clouds
Illuminate by emeralds hidden in the grass
Wake up in blades
The yellow magnified by 10
Amazement at such perfect construction
Genetic marvels
The mind flits about
Soaking inward the energy
Filling deeply needed bones
Rich to glowing
Wrapped, swirl fine silk butter mantle about
My body around over under closed
Spring meal blessings me

Down Filled

I fly like cottonwood down
As indirect as possible
Wrung out like wet clothes
Untangling the twisted
Lost in the damp
Mind spinning onward

Elemental

The wind stirs the tree on hill
Swish about in bursts
Playing catch with the sky
That changes from gray to blue
The day-long gray is breaking up
The wet earth humid drawn
In lines of green
Emerald, celery, neon, lime
Sings unfolds curled hand to blow a kiss
To still the mind
And hold the body
Let the elements sweep past
Clean the debris at long last
Nudge into the sublime
Twirl in circle each crevice exposed
To fill again with joy
The smell of rich soil
The isolated drops of rain
Form the overloaded lone cloud
Surprise the face caress the cheek
And back the sun to heat the deep
Mysterious imaginations of you

I am the element of air fleeting
Dashing past
Racing on
Parachute of body flown
Encompass the north winds song, warm sweet humid direction fly
Elemental body I

About Atmosphere Press

Atmosphere Press is an independent, full-service publisher for excellent books in all genres and for all audiences. Learn more about what we do at atmospherepress.com.

We encourage you to check out some of Atmosphere's latest releases, which are available at Amazon.com and via order from your local bookstore:

About the Author

Tricia Johnson is a poet wishing to share her work with others, using the written word to embrace the essence of life. She is a retired teacher. She lives in the beautiful hills of Pennsylvania with her husband and two sons. Her published work includes the poem "Living with Lupus" which appeared in *Still You Poems of Illness & Healing,* Wolf Ridge Press 2020, and her debut book of poems, *Whirl Away Girl*, published by Atmosphere Press in 2021.